On the Move

WELDON OWEN PTY LTD
Publisher: Sheena Coupe
Senior Designer: Kylie Mulquin
Editorial Coordinators: Sarah Anderson,
Tracey Gibson
Production Manager: Helen Creeke
Production Assistant: Kylie Lawson

Project Editor: Ariana Klepac
Designer: Patricia Ansell
Text: Jan Stradling

05 04 03 02 01 00
10 9 8 7 6 5 4 3 2 1

Published in New Zealand by Shortland Publications,
2B Cawley Street, Ellerslie, Auckland.
Published in the United Kingdom by
Kingscourt Publishing Limited,
P.O. Box 1427, Freepost, London W6 9BR.
Published in Australia by Shortland-Mimosa,
8 Yarra Street, Hawthorn, Victoria 3122.

Printed in Singapore
ISBN: 0-7699-1260-5

CREDITS AND ACKNOWLEDGMENTS

PICTURE AND ILLUSTRATION CREDITS
[t=top, b=bottom, l=left, r=right, c=centre]
Corbis 14b. **Corel Corp.** 8b. **Dan Cole/Wildlife Art Ltd.** 4-5c. **B. Croucher/Wildlife Art Ltd.** 4b, 6. **Lloyd Foye** 8-9b.
Ray Grinaway 9t, 13b. **David Kirshner** 1, 5b, 7, 11c, 15. **John Mac/ FOLIO** 5t, 16. **Rob Mancini** 3t, 11t. **Photodisc** banding.
Trevor Ruth 12-13. **P.Scott/Wildlife Art Ltd.** 3b, 10b, 15. **Kevin Stead** 13t. **Roger Swainston** 11b.

Weldon Owen would like to thank the following people for their assistance in the production of this book:
Peta Gorman, Michael Hann, Marney Richardson.

Contents

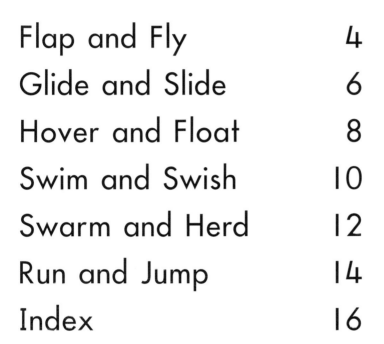

Flap and Fly

Birds and some other animals have wings that help them travel through the sky. Some birds fly all the way across the world.

Birds flap their wings to help them stay in the air and to push them through the air.

Bats have wings.
The wings are
made of skin.

Geese

A flying fish has
wing-shaped fins that help
it glide across the water.

An albatross glides
through the air.

Glide and Slide

Some birds and animals have
big wings that help them glide
through the air. Some animals
slide across the ground.

The flying
squirrel glides
from tree
to tree.

A snake
wriggles its body
to slide across
the ground.

Hover and Float

Some birds and insects have wings that they can flap very quickly. This helps them hover in one place in the air.

Dragonfly

Dragonflies can
flap their wings
up to 50 times
per second.

A hummingbird flaps
its wings so quickly
that they make
a humming sound.

Swim and Swish

Fish have fins and tails to help them swim. Some other animals have special features that help them move through the water.

Penguins are birds that cannot fly.
They use their wings like flippers.

Some birds have webbed feet. They use their feet like paddles.

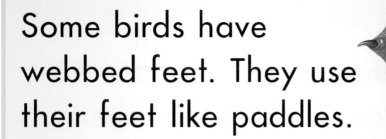

Crocodiles use their tails to help them swim.

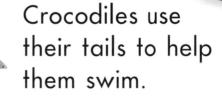

A shark's tail helps it move forward.

Swarm and Herd

Some animals travel together in big groups. This helps them to look after one another.

Some ants can fly.
They travel together
in a swarm.

Bees in a swarm

Run and Jump

Many animals have strong legs that help them to run quickly. Some animals can jump high into the air.

White-tailed deer

The cheetah
has long legs
and is the fastest animal
in the world.

Ostrich
45 mph
(72 km/h)

Racehorse
43 mph
(70 km/h)

Adult male
22 mph
(36 km/h)

Index